D1156243

# AMAZING STRUCTURES
# DAMS

by Rebecca Pettiford

# Ideas for Parents and Teachers

Pogo Books let children practice reading informational text while introducing them to nonfiction features such as headings, labels, sidebars, maps, and diagrams, as well as a table of contents, glossary, and index.

Carefully leveled text with a strong photo match offers early fluent readers the support they need to succeed.

## Before Reading

- "Walk" through the book and point out the various nonfiction features. Ask the student what purpose each feature serves.
- Look at the glossary together. Read and discuss the words.

## Read the Book

- Have the child read the book independently.
- Invite him or her to list questions that arise from reading.

## After Reading

- Discuss the child's questions. Talk about how he or she might find answers to those questions.
- Prompt the child to think more. Ask: What is the biggest dam you have ever seen?

Pogo Books are published by Jump!
5357 Penn Avenue South
Minneapolis, MN 55419
www.jumplibrary.com

Library of Congress Cataloging-in-Publication Data

Pettiford, Rebecca, author.
 Dams / by Rebecca Pettiford.
  pages cm. – (Amazing structures)
 Audience: Ages 7-9.
 Includes bibliographical reference and index.
 ISBN 978-1-62031-213-1 (hardcover: alk. paper) –
 ISBN 978-1-62496-300-1 (ebook)
 1. Dams–Juvenile literature.  I. Title.
 TC540.P43 2016
 627.8–dc23

                                    2014042534

Series Editor: Jenny Fretland VanVoorst
Series Designer: Anna Peterson
Photo Researcher: Anna Peterson

Photo Credits: All photos by Shutterstock except: Corbis, 16-17; Getty, 18, 19; Thinkstock, 10–11, 12-13.

Printed in the United States of America at Corporate Graphics in North Mankato, Minnesota.

# TABLE OF CONTENTS

# CHAPTER 1

· · · · · · · · · · · · · · · · · · · · · · · · · · · · · · · · · · · · · · · · · · · · · · · · · · · · ·

# WHAT IS A DAM?

We cannot live without water. That's why we build dams.

People have been building dams for more than 4,000 years.

A dam is a large structure that holds water in place. It creates a secure, reliable water supply. The water that gathers on one side of the dam is called a **reservoir**.

reservoir

Water weighs a lot. To control it, dams need to be large and strong.

There are several types of dams. Some are made from **concrete**. Others are made of earth.

How do we use dams? Let's find out.

# CHAPTER 2

# HOW DO WE USE DAMS?

By controlling the flow of water, a dam can prevent flooding.

It can direct water to farmland.

Drinking water often comes from a reservoir.

generator

Dams can use water to make electricity. This is called **hydroelectricity**.

The force of the water turns blades in a **turbine**. The turbine then turns a **generator**. The generator makes electricity, which can power your house!

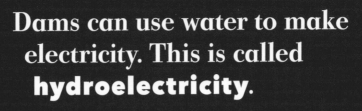
TAKE A LOOK!

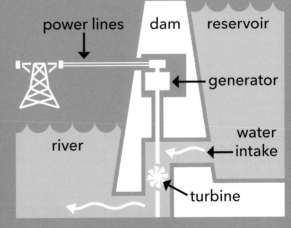

How can a dam turn water into power? Look inside!

power lines   dam   reservoir

generator

river   water intake

turbine

Changes in a river's water level can make it hard for boats to **navigate**.

A dam can keep a river's water level steady.

How does it do this?

It uses **locks** and **spillways**.

STOP

NO BOATING ALLOWED
WITHIN 100 YARDS OF DAM
WHEN GATES ARE OPEN

A U.S.C.G. Approved Life Jacket
Must Be Worn Within 100 Yds. of Dam
(Garland County Ordinance #0-93-15)

◄ • • • • • • spillway

A lock is a gated waterway built alongside a dam. When a boat enters, the gates close. Depending on which way the boat is going, the water level goes up or down.

To keep the water depth steady, spillways open and close to let water through.

gates

spillway

Dams often have more than one use.

The Oroville Dam in California supplies water and power. It also controls floods. It is 770 feet (235 meters) tall. That's about as tall as 200 second graders standing on top of one another!

# CHAPTER 3

. . . . . . . . . . . . . . . . . . . . . . . . . . . . . . . . . . . . . . .

# BUILDING DAMS

**Civil engineers** build dams. They learn how much water the dam needs to support.

They decide how big and strong it needs to be. If a dam cracks or wears away, they repair it.

There's no doubt that a dam has made your life better.

Your drinking water may come from a reservoir. Your food may come from an **irrigated** farm. Your house may run on hydroelectricity.

One day you may build a dam!

# ACTIVITIES & TOOLS

## BUILD A DAM

**In this activity, you will build a dam.**
**You will need the following materials:**

- a long, shallow plastic container
- sand
- rocks and sticks
- a bucket of water

**❶ Fill your container with sand.**
**Dig a path in the sand.**
**This is your "river."**

**❷ Pick a spot along your river to build your dam.**

**❸ Use rocks and sticks to build the dam. Make sure that a little water will be able to pass through.**

**❹ If the water is deep, the water pressure will be higher. This means the bottom of the dam must hold more pressure. It will need to be wider at the bottom.**

**❺ It's time to see how strong your dam is. Take your bucket and slowly pour water down your river.**

**❻ What happened? Did your dam hold most of the water back? Did you need to make changes in its design?**

# GLOSSARY

**civil engineers:** People who design and build dams and other structures.

**concrete:** A mix of broken stone or gravel, sand, cement, and water, that hardens after it is spread or poured.

**generator:** A machine that changes energy into electricity.

**hydroelectricity:** Electricity that is created by using the energy of moving water.

**irrigate:** To supply water to land and crops.

**lock:** A section of waterway in which the water level can be lowered or raised by opening and closing gates.

**navigate:** To plan and direct the course of a boat, ship, plane, or other form of transportation.

**reservoir:** A large lake on one side of a dam that is used as a supply source for water.

**spillway:** A passage in a dam that releases water.

**turbine:** A machine in which a wheel with blades is made to turn by fast-moving water.

## INDEX

## TO LEARN MORE

Learning more is as easy as 1, 2, 3.

1) Go to www.factsurfer.com

2) Enter "dams" into the search box.

3) Click the "Surf" to see a list of websites.

With factsurfer, finding more information is just a click away.